DETECTIVE
DAN
&The Missing Toy Boat

MARQUES LEWIS
ILLUSTRATED BY: GARRETT MYERS

DETECTIVE DAN

&The Missing Toy Boat

This book is dedicated to my family, friends and to all of the kids who love Detective Dan.

You rock!

It's getting late, and it was almost Dan's bedtime.
"Dan! Dan! Dan! Time to take a bath!

Grab one toy and get in the tub." Mom yelled!

Dan and Justin Beaver are having so much fun playing with Dan's toy cars.

"OK MOM!" Dan said.

"Hmmm...What toy do I want to play with Justin? I know!" Dan said while jumping into his toy box.

He DUG! DUG! DUG!
He couldn't find what he was looking for.

He began to think long and hard.
"Where's my toy boat?"

...Now that's a MYSTERY.

"This looks like a job for Detective Dan and Detective Beaver!"

All I need is my **maggy glass, my jacket** and **my hat.**
I can solve any mystery just like that."
Dan said while posing in his detective outfit.

"Dan, hurry and get in the tub
before your water gets cold!"
His mom yelled from the kitchen.
"Ok mom!" Dan replied.

We don't have much time to solve this mystery.
I don't remember where I had it last," Dan said,
while looking at the empty clue board.

Dan searched **HIGH** and **LOW,** from the wall to the floor,

but couldn't find what he was looking for.

As Dan searched the room, he found his first clue,
a track of wet foot prints.

They followed to see where they led to.
"Hey! They're coming from mom's room.

As time winds down, he continued following the tracks that led to mom's bathroom. "I REMEMBER NOW! "He yelled excitedly.

"I played with it earlier in mom's sink. Hurry Justin, we are out of time!"

"Dan! Times up! You better be in the tub,"
Mom said, while opening the bathroom door.

"Look at you! You've been busy,"
Mom said, watching Dan goof off.

THE END!

Your turn to become a detective

GAMES & ACTIVITIES

Dan and Justin lost their color, can you help them find there color?
Fill in there color by using the clue chart on the side .

Clue chart

Grey	1
Orange	2
Red	3
Green	4
Brown	5
White	6
Peach	7

Fill in the color of the boat using the clue chart at the bottom .

MISSING BOAT

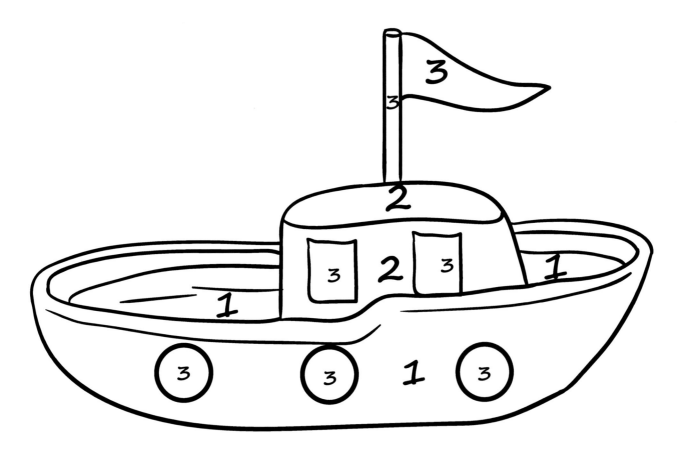

Clue chart

Yellow	1
Orange	2
Blue	3

Dan wants to play with his toy boat for bathtime, except he can't find it. Help Dan find his Toy boat.

Start

MARQUES LEWIS

About The Author

Marques Lewis (30 years old) was born in Newark, New Jersey and raised until 12 years old in Irvington, New Jersey. He is an best-selling author of 17 books. He won the 2013 "Best-Selling" Award at One Karma Publishing Award show. Marques wrote Detective Dan: "The Missing Toy Boat" at the age of seven. Marques has his own publishing company called Marvelous Leaders Publications. You can find Marques' novels on www.amazon.com and www.goodreads.com. His novels on Kindle, the Amazon Kindle app, and paperback as well. You can add Marques on Facebook at Author Marques Lewis, Twitter, Instagram @iammarqueslewis, and his websitewww.iammarqueslewis.com. You can also reach him at his email address marques.lewis@aol.com.

About the Illustrator - Garrett Myers

Garrett resides in Albany, Georgia. He has been drawing since he was a little boy. He is gifted and talented and uses his gifts and talents to glorify God in all that he draws. He always reminds others that his drawings are creations from God, and his tools are His handiworks.

Contacts:
Garrettmyersart@gmail.com
kreatedjustforyou@gmail.com

Made in the USA
Middletown, DE
30 August 2022